Woods**Walk**

STOREY KIDS Storey Books

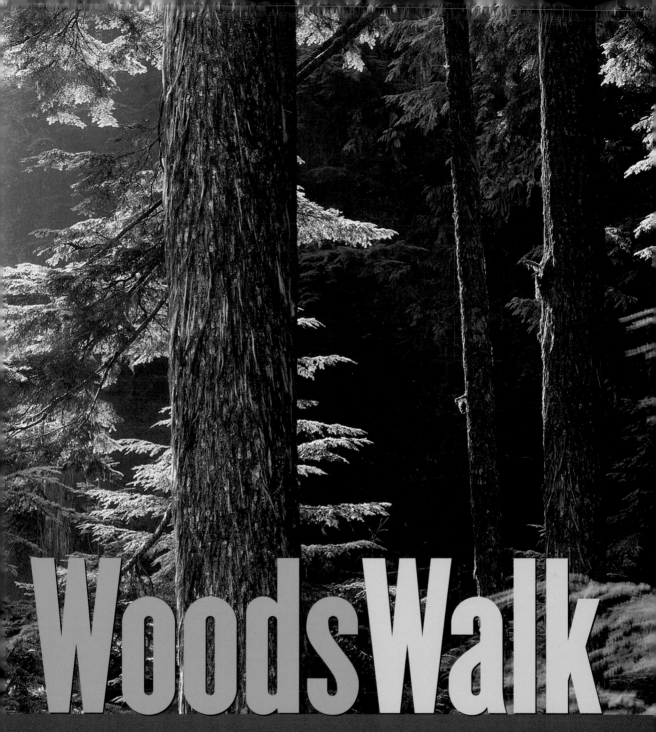

WoodsWalk

Peepers, porcupines & exploding puffballs!
What you'll see, hear & smell when exploring the woods.

Henry W. Art and Michael W. Robbins

To Maisy.
May the woods always be a source of joy. — H.A.

The mission of Storey Publishing is to serve our customers by publishing practical information that encourages personal independence in harmony with the environment.

Edited by Anne Kostick and Deborah Burns
Designed by Wendy Palitz and Elizabeth Johnsboen
Text production by Stephen Hughes and Kelley Nesbit
Illustrations by Clare Walker Leslie except as noted on page 118
Cover Photographs: Back cover bottom right © CORBIS; front cover center © Ed
  Gifford/Masterfile; back cover top right © Anne Gordon; front cover top left Giles
  Prett; front cover bottom left © Rob Simpson/PAINET; back cover top left and bottom left
  © David Westphalen/PAINET
Spy Guide illustrations by Ilona Sherratt
Interior photography and illustration credits on page 118
Indexed by Peggy Holloway

The information in this book is true and complete to the best of our knowledge. All recommendations are made without guarantee on the part of the author or Storey Publishing. The author and publisher disclaim any liability in connection with the use of this information. For additional information please contact Storey Books, 210 MASS MoCA Way, North Adams, MA 01247.

Storey books are available for special premium and promotional uses and for customized editions. For further information, please call Storey's Custom Publishing Department at 1-800-793-9396.

Printed in China by Regent Publishing Services
10 9 8 7 6 5 4 3 2 1

Library of Congress Cataloging-in-Publication Data

Art, Henry Warren.
   Woodswalk : peepers, porcupines, and exploding puffballs / Henry W. Art and Michael W.
   Robbins.
      p. cm.
   Summary: Describes the different animals and plants one can see on a
   walk through the woods during the four seasons.
   Includes index and bibliographical references (p.   ).
   ISBN 1-58017-452-3 (pbk. : alk. paper) — ISBN 1-58017-477-9
   (hardcover : alk. paper)
   1. Forest animals—Juvenile literature. 2. Forest plants—Juvenile
   literature. 3. Nature study—Juvenile literature. [1. Forest animals.
   2. Forest plants. 3. Nature study. 4. Seasons.] I. Robbins, Michael W.
   II. Title.
QH86.A84 2003
508.352—dc21
                    2002010514

contents

What Is a Forest?

At first you may think of woods as dark and scary places, filled with creepy animals and frightening sounds. Or they may seem ordinary to you — just a lot of green trees and shrubs, and maybe some bugs, but not a place where much happens.

Once you come to know them, however, forests are enchanting, busy places. There is much more going on in the woods, and there are many more creatures — large and small and even tiny — living there than you will see, hear, smell, or feel at first.

A forest is an area of trees growing close enough to each other that their tops overlap, shading the ground below. But it is much more than that. It is a community of living things that have all grown up together. The plants, animals, birds, fungi, bacteria, and other creatures have adjusted to one another. Over many years and many generations, each living thing from the smallest bacterium to the tallest tree has adapted, or changed, in order to survive and thrive in its surroundings.

Being Green

Chlorophyll, a chemical compound that appears green (and gives leaves their summer color), is the major substance found in nature that can turn the energy of sunlight into another form of energy. Plants use chlorophyll to convert sunlight into glucose, a food they can use to grow.

A Squirrel is an Oak Tree's Best Friend

Squirrels eat acorns, which contain the seeds of oak trees. In autumn, squirrels hide a lot of acorns to use as food during the winter, but they usually forget where they buried some. The "lost" acorns sprout the next spring. This helps oak trees spread, as those forgotten acorns grow into more oak trees and make more acorns for squirrels to eat.

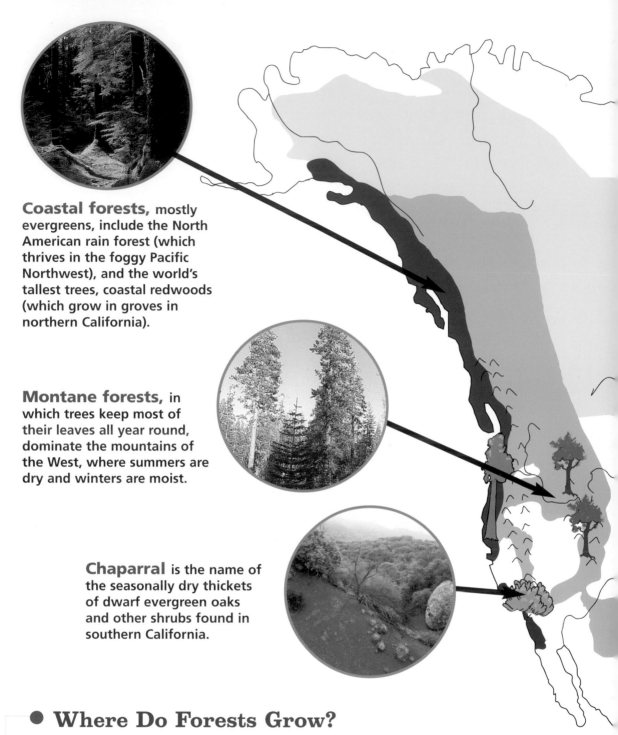

Coastal forests, mostly evergreens, include the North American rain forest (which thrives in the foggy Pacific Northwest), and the world's tallest trees, coastal redwoods (which grow in groves in northern California).

Montane forests, in which trees keep most of their leaves all year round, dominate the mountains of the West, where summers are dry and winters are moist.

Chaparral is the name of the seasonally dry thickets of dwarf evergreen oaks and other shrubs found in southern California.

● Where Do Forests Grow?

Forests grow where the ground is moist during the growing season and where droughts and other major disturbances are rare. The East has plenty of rain and snow throughout the year, but in the West the summers are dry and trees depend on water stored in the soil. Grasslands are found where moisture is uneven, fires are frequent, and grazing animals are common.

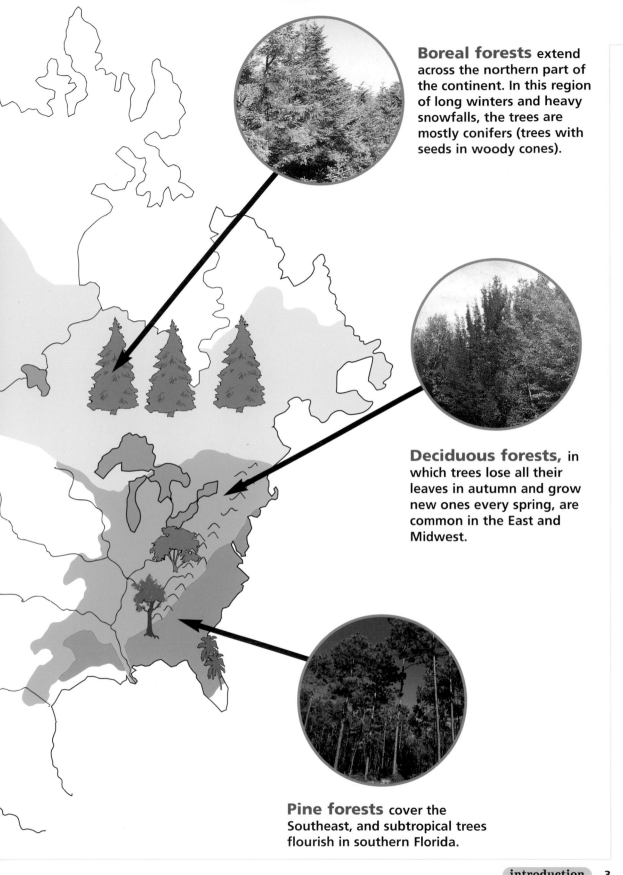

Boreal forests extend across the northern part of the continent. In this region of long winters and heavy snowfalls, the trees are mostly conifers (trees with seeds in woody cones).

Deciduous forests, in which trees lose all their leaves in autumn and grow new ones every spring, are common in the East and Midwest.

Pine forests cover the Southeast, and subtropical trees flourish in southern Florida.

● The Lives of a Forest

A forest grows and changes over time. As it grows, some kinds of plants and trees flourish while others die off. As the plants and trees change, different animals come to live there. Often, a forest changes because of a big natural disturbance like a flood, volcanic eruption, insect swarm, ice storm, hurricane, avalanche, forest fire, or human activity such as clear-cutting or agriculture.

Forest fire! When a large fire sweeps through a forest, burning nearly everything living, it sets off changes that may take hundreds of years to complete.

First to return. Certain species of pine trees and other conifers are most likely to survive the fire, thanks to their thick bark, their ability to resprout, and their cones, which open in response to heat. Aspens soon join them in repopulating the woods. Windblown seeds arrive and quickly sprout.

Growth spurt. With so many trees burned, sunlight can reach all the way to the ground and help the pines and other sun-loving plants, such as wood aster and fireweed, grow and thrive.

Hardwoods catch up. In the East, deciduous trees such as maple, oak, ash, and hickory begin to grow up. They cast shade on the pines and aspens, slowing their growth.

Full circle. Finally, the hardwoods become the main kind of trees in the forest — until the next fire.

Plants and Plant Eaters

Green plants use chlorophyll to capture energy from the sun, which helps them make wood, branches, bark, and leaves. They also produce chemicals that make them taste bad to many of the plant-eating animals (called *herbivores*) that might otherwise eat them.

Dead plant parts that fall to the ground are food for many insects, fungi, and microbes known as *detritivores*.

Energy Flows

When any living thing dies, it is consumed by tiny decomposers. Small animals eat those tiny creatures and are in turn eaten by larger ones. The arrows below show the directions the energy flows in this natural cycle.

Predators and Prey

Many animals, large and small, kill and eat other animals. The ones that get eaten are called *prey* and those that do the killing and eating are called *predators*. Both are important in a woods community. Without predators, there would be too many prey animals and not enough food for them all. Without prey, there would not be enough food for the predators and they might die off. A healthy community strikes a balance between predators and prey.

Some prey animals, such as the American toad, defend themselves by hiding and holding still. Their coloring makes them hard to see against the forest floor. They also taste terrible. Others, like rabbits and whitetail deer, defend themselves by fleeing. Some defend themselves by fighting back with horns or antlers, hooves, sharp claws, or teeth. Skunks defend themselves by their awful smell, porcupines defend themselves with sharp quills, opossums by playing dead, and woodchucks by fleeing into a deep burrow.

Nearly every animal has natural enemies that it tries to avoid or fight off. Small creatures like insects are preyed upon by larger animals like amphibians and songbirds, which are in turn preyed upon by even larger animals like raptors and coyotes. Many animals are both predator and prey.

cottontail rabbit

Hiding in Plain Sight

In most forests, you'll find many different animals with similar brown and black coloring and mottled patterns in skin, fur, and feathers. This *camouflage* allows them to blend into the forest background so they are hard to spot by predators . . . and by human woodswalkers like you. Keep a sharp eye out for creatures wearing camouflage.

Red fox eating a pheasant.

● Getting into the Woods

Sometimes you'll decide to go woodswalking on the spur of the moment. Other times you'll be able to plan your walk. Either way, it helps to have woodswalking smarts — learn what to bring, what to wear, and how to behave in the woods.

Bring a map, if you can, and learn how to read it. If you're walking in a state or national park or wildlife sanctuary, try to find a map that shows exactly where you're going — all trails and important landmarks should be on the map. The best map of all is a contour map, usually called a seven-and-a-half-minute map or a United States Geologic Survey (USGS) map. These maps are produced by the U.S. government and are usually sold at hiking, backpacking, and fishing and hunting stores.

Check the weather and season. The weather report will help you decide how to dress for your walk. And learning about what to expect in each season in the woods will help you plan your walk. Also, check in your area for the dates of hunting seasons. Don't walk in the woods during deer-, elk-, or bear-hunting season.

Go with a friend and tell an adult where you are going and which route you are taking. Young children should always go woodswalking with an adult.

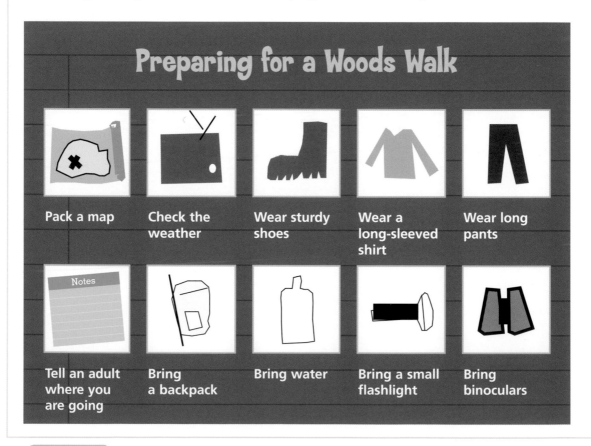

Preparing for a Woods Walk

| Pack a map | Check the weather | Wear sturdy shoes | Wear a long-sleeved shirt | Wear long pants |
| Tell an adult where you are going | Bring a backpack | Bring water | Bring a small flashlight | Bring binoculars |

Go Slow

It's a walk in the woods, not a race or a survival contest. You can have a lot of fun and sense a lot of what's happening in a forest in just a mile or so. In fact, the more slowly you move, the more you will see, hear, and smell.

Some trails — especially in places like national or state forests or wildlife refuges — have been cleared and marked just for hiking. They often have small signs identifying the trail, and many have *blazes*, or rectangular paint marks, about 6 feet off the ground on older trees. Above the tree line, trails may be marked by *cairns*, small heaps of stones. **Be sure to stay on the trail.**

How should you behave in the woods? Try acting truly like an animal. Animals in the woods are as observant and quiet as they can be. Their lives depend upon it, and that is why it's rare to spot more than a few of them. You will hear and see more by quietly watching and listening. Many hikers follow the practice of leaving only footprints and taking only memories (or notes or photographs). A forest is not the place to advertise your presence. And remember — whatever you pack into a forest, pack it out when you leave.

A forest is a fragile environment. Don't pick or break or mark anything. Instead, observe closely and try to sense the movements and changes and patterns of things all around you.

On a United States Geologic Survey (USGS) map, forests are green, open space is tan, and contour lines show elevation above sea level.

Poisonous Trio

Learn to identify these plants, then stay away from them.

Poison ivy: Clusters of three shiny pointed leaves, with white berries. Grows as a vine, on the ground, or as a shrub. Likes damp areas. Every part of it exudes an oil very irritating to human skin.

Poison oak: Very similar to poison ivy but with blunt, slightly hairy leaves. Found mostly in southern and western woodlands.

Poison sumac: A shrub or small tree, even more irritating than the other two but far less common and usually found only in swamps.

Wildflower Warning

Look, but do not pick the wildflowers. Unlike garden flowers, they are very fragile and will wilt before you can get them home. And these plants may die off if the flowers are picked; they need the blossoms to produce the fruits that contain their seeds.

Plant Warnings

Do not touch **devil's club.** It has huge maplelike leaves, and its stems are covered with spiky thorns.

Also avoid the large leaves of **cowparsnip.** Although the leaves are smooth, they can cause blistering on sensitive skin.

Tick Talk

Tiny, pale or brown, and often hard to see, **ticks** lurk on grasses and shrubs and jump aboard any passing warm body — a deer, a dog, even you. Then they bite. You won't feel the bite, but unfortunately, ticks can transfer diseases with their bite. The most dangerous one is Lyme disease, commonly carried by deer ticks, which are no larger than the period that ends this sentence. Use insect repellent and wear long sleeves and long pants. When you return from your walk, check your arms, legs, and neck for tiny tick passengers.

● The Reason for Seasons

A rainy spring, a hot dry summer, an early autumn frost, a long cold winter: The North American woods are strongly affected by the changing seasons. Because the earth is tilted as it makes its long journey around the sun, different parts of the globe receive different amounts of light and warmth. That's why we have seasons.

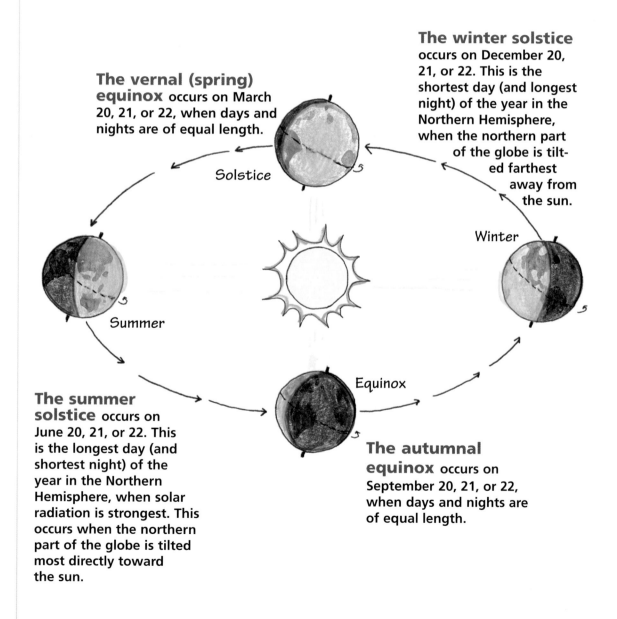

The winter solstice occurs on December 20, 21, or 22. This is the shortest day (and longest night) of the year in the Northern Hemisphere, when the northern part of the globe is tilted farthest away from the sun.

The vernal (spring) equinox occurs on March 20, 21, or 22, when days and nights are of equal length.

Solstice

Winter

Summer

The summer solstice occurs on June 20, 21, or 22. This is the longest day (and shortest night) of the year in the Northern Hemisphere, when solar radiation is strongest. This occurs when the northern part of the globe is tilted most directly toward the sun.

Equinox

The autumnal equinox occurs on September 20, 21, or 22, when days and nights are of equal length.

spr

Spring is when the woods wake up and "spring" to life. The days are growing longer; after the spring equinox they are longer than the nights. The sun rises higher as it crosses the sky and here, north of the equator, its rays are striking the earth at a steeper angle. With stronger sunlight, the air, soil, and everything else in the woods can warm up after the long chill of winter.

New life. Fawns, born in late spring, are carefully hidden by their mothers in the woods. Completely odorless and well camouflaged, they are safe from predators.

Trees that lose their leaves (*deciduous* trees) have been inactive, or dormant, during the cold winter. Reptiles and some mammals hibernate during the winter. Many others, from raccoons and skunks to black bears, sleep the winter away, rousing themselves for only a short time each day. In spring they awaken.

Many species begin life in the spring, mating or giving birth. Some birds stay in the northern forests year-round, but many more arrive in migrating flocks, along with the warm weather from the South. Spring is a time to look and listen for signs of new life and activity in the woods.

Spring Weather Report

💧 Spring moves north like a wave of warmth, traveling at an average of 32 miles per day. It arrives first in forests, then in meadows, and finally in wetlands.

💧 In all regions, days are longer than nights, but nights can still be very chilly.

💧 In the East, warm weather alternates with cool and cold weather.

💧 The Rockies experience hot downslope winds called **chinooks.** Farther west, it's foggy and mild or cool on the coast and warm inland.

💧 Throughout the West it still feels like winter at high elevations, but it is warm on clear, sunny days.

What's Up?

Check out what these three creatures are doing in spring.

Black bears emerge from their dens with new cubs that were born while their mothers were sleeping during the winter.

Cecropia moths emerge from cocoons in mid-spring. The adults never eat; they breed and then die.

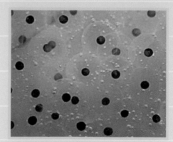

Wood frogs come out of hibernation and mate very early in spring, the males calling from vernal pools. The females lay masses of jellylike eggs.

East

In a leafless eastern forest in the early spring, the increasing sunlight reaches down to the forest floor and warms the soil and the organisms living there. Their moment in the sun may last only a few weeks, however, especially for wildflowers. After the treetops leaf out, the creatures and plants beneath them will live in shade. The forest changes rapidly as the shade increases and the days grow warm.

When spring snow melts under the sun, it runs down to fill streams, form the temporary ponds and puddles known as *vernal pools* (above), and just soak into the soil. Without a canopy of leaves to block the rain, it falls straight to the forest floor, keeping everything nice and moist.

● Spring Shapes and Colors

In early spring it's easy to notice the different shapes of the trees. The colors of early spring are still mostly drab browns and grays. Evergreens provide some strong color — a white pine, for example, with its long dark green needles. Look at the treetops to find some other colors. The red maple is named not just for its dark red leaves in fall, but also for its reddish buds and flowers in early spring. Those buds create a reddish haze in the pattern of the twigs. Look for these bright red buds and then the popcorn-sized flowers before the leaves appear.

red maple
flowers

Paper birches have purplish brown buds and white bark.

Poplars have greenish bark and yellow-green *catkins* (clusters of petal-less buds).

Red maple flowers look like red popcorn on gray twigs in early spring.

Willows have yellow-green buds on yellow, red, or brown twigs.

eastern redbud

Below the tallest treetops, you'll see shorter trees and shrubs (the *under-story*) in the most sunlight they'll receive until next fall. Some, like redbuds, flowering dogwood, and shadbush, bloom before the taller trees leaf out. Young oaks, maples, and beeches stand with their leaves fanned out, soaking up the sunlight they need to grow. Later in spring they'll be in the shade of the older, taller trees.

Bug Box

You may glimpse a pillbug on the ground. It looks as if it's wearing a suit of armor, and it rolls itself into a tight ball at the first hint of danger. Also known as sowbugs or wood lice, pillbugs eat mostly dead plants and animals.

● Nests and Nest Builders

Once they pair off and mate, birds nest almost every-where in the forest, from the ground to the tops of the tallest trees. Most of the birds you'll see in the eastern forests build their nests after the *canopy trees* (the tallest trees) have leafed out. To spot a new nest, watch for a bird flying with nesting materials clutched in its beak: twigs, stems, bits of vine or leaf, mosses, feathers, and even bits of string or paper if it happens to find them. Keep your eye on the bird to see where it goes.

robin's nest

Nest Spotter

If you find a nest, please look but do not touch or disturb it. The mother is probably nearby, waiting for you to move on.

BIRD	NEST LOCATION	MATERIALS
ruffed grouse	on the ground	pine needles, grass, and leaves
wild turkey	base of a tree or concealed in grass	a loose batch of ferns and leaves
duck	on the ground	large, down-lined
eastern towhee	dense brush, usually within five feet of the ground	weeds, bark, grass, hair, to form an open cup
wood thrushes, robins, and blue jays	higher up, on horizontal branches of shrubs and low trees	cup-shaped, mud-and-grass
woodpeckers, nuthatches, and chickadees	excavated cavities well up in standing dead trees, with entrance often disguised	usually made of grasses, mosses, bark fibers
warblers	nearly anywhere from ground level to treetop	usually an open cup of grasses, weeds, mosses, bark fibers

After spending the winter in warmer waters, **Canada geese** may appear in a ragged V, high in the sky, heading north to summer lakes. A cascade of nasal honks may float down to earth if you're quiet enough to hear it.

The low drumming that sounds like a motor starting up, getting faster and faster, is made by a male **ruffed grouse.** He beats the air with his wings to attract the attention of any female grouse in the area.

● Shhhh

To many forms of life — animals, birds, and insects — motion and noise mean *danger.* They won't move if they hear or see you moving. When you're quiet for a few minutes and really listen to the woods, you'll notice sounds you might miss while tramping along and talking.

Even in early spring you may hear flocks of migrating birds traveling from their warmer winter ground toward their breeding territories in the North.

Birdsong Basics

Here are some songs and calls you might hear in the woods on a spring morning.

Blue Jay: "Jay, jay,"; "beadle, beadle"

Chickadee: "Chickadee-dee-dee"

Wood Thrush: "Ee-o-lay"

Veery: "Veer, veer, veer"

Robin: "Cheery-up, cheery-up"

Cardinal: "Birdie, birdie, birdie"

Yellow-rumped Warbler: "Tcheck"

Ovenbird: "Teacher, teacher, teacher"

Early Birds

Although humans prefer to hike at mid-day, many birds are more active at the first light of dawn. Sunrise is their signal to be up and searching for food. So the earlier you take your walk, the more birds you will hear as they sing to define their territories, warn off competitors, and attract mates.

yellow-rumped
warbler

Blackbirds, for example, make a lot of noise when a large flock of them — grackles, red-winged blackbirds, and brown-headed cowbirds — suddenly settles into the treetops.

Warblers are tiny and colorful migrating birds. But of the 20 or so different species that visit the eastern woods, only the yellow-rumped (myrtle) warbler is likely to be spotted in early spring. That's because it likes bayberries and other berries as much as it likes the insects that will appear later. Listen for its thin, warbling song or its surprisingly loud *tcheck!*

If you hear a light, hollow, rhythmic tapping in the trees, it may be a downy woodpecker. The smallest and most widespread of all woodpeckers, it pounds its bill into tree trunks, seeking beetles and other insects.

Opossums sleep during the day and may pretend to be dead when frightened. Young possums can hang from branches by their tails, but they lose this ability as they grow older.

A porcupine chewed off this bark to eat it during the winter. Look for patches of missing bark with the telltale shallow grooves that resemble chisel marks.

Beavers fell pondside trees, cut up the branches, drag them to the water, and store them in their lodges.

● Who's There?

White-tailed deer, opossums, skunks, porcupines, and other mammals rely on the cover of darkness while feeding and moving about. You're more likely to see or hear them in the faint light of dawn or in the evening.

At a beaver dam and pond, evening is the best time to observe the busy lives of these surprisingly large (50- to 100-pound) rodents. It's a good idea to sneak up on beavers. If one hears you, it will slap its tail on the water to warn its lodge mates and then dive.

Treasures Underfoot

Revisit the woods every couple of weeks during the spring. You'll see trees and low shrubs begin to leaf out, changing the light. Wildflowers will be blooming, many of them with easily noticed white or yellow blossoms.

Yellow sessile bellwort, with its drooping flowers, likes shady woods.

Tall lousewort has clustered red and yellow blossoms.

The giant trillium has a single, wide, three-part flower that is white at first and then turns pink or purplish.

Trout lilies may be blooming, with their pointed yellow blossoms and mottled leaves that resemble a trout's patchy color pattern.

Ferns may be unfolding their new fronds, called fiddleheads.

Morels, mushrooms with ridged and pitted caps, may be emerging.

Take one whiff and you'll know how skunk cabbage earned its name.

Night Walks

On a spring night, one of the loudest sounds you'll hear comes from one of the smallest amphibians — the spring peeper. It's a high trilling whistle with a rising note, usually heard in a chorus. Peepers breed in vernal pools, temporary ponds that form from melting snow and spring rains and dry up in the heat of summer. Peepers and other amphibians — toads, frogs, and salamanders — are in a race to grow up before the vernal pools dry out.

Peepers cling to trees near water, and they sing mostly at night. Look for a pond or swampy area during daylight, then return to it at night with an adult, preferably after a rain, and follow the sound of the

peepers. Bring a flashlight for safe walking. When the peepers hear you, they will fall silent, but if you turn off your flashlight and stand still in the darkness for a few minutes, they'll begin singing again. When you are close to the pond or swamp, shine your light on some nearby trees, and you may spot the peepers. They are small, only about an inch long, and their color varies from tan and gray to orange.

While you are pausing for the peepers, listen carefully for other night sounds, including wood frogs (more of a quack than a song). Listen for screech owls, which do not screech, but instead give a long, soft, descending, and rather mournful wail; or a great horned owl, which delivers deep "hoots," often five at a time. Barred owls sound as if they're asking "Who, who, who cooks for you?"

"peep·peep"

"squck·squck"

West

Spring is different in the West, especially in the high mountains of the Sierra Nevada, the Rockies, and other ranges. In the colder mountain heights the winter's snowpack may linger so long that taking a spring walk in the woods is simply impossible — unless you're wearing snowshoes! But in these woods, once the snow melts, winter rapidly turns into summer.

Forests vary more widely in the West than in the East, so what you'll see, hear, and smell will depend on whether you're walking in the Pacific Northwest, on the middle Pacific coast, or higher up in the mountains inland, and whether you're on the west slope or the east slope.

Wind and weather generally move from west to east. When the air meets the high mountain ranges, which generally run north and south, it cools as it is forced upward. Cooler air cannot hold as much moisture as warm air can, which means that it rains a lot on the western slopes of mountains such as the Sierra Nevada and the Rocky Mountains. The rain turns to snow higher up, so much that it's measured in feet, not inches. The eastern slopes of the mountains lie in a "rain shadow" and receive much less rain and snow.

Eastbound winds dump rain and snow on the western slopes of the Sierra Nevada and the Rockies, leaving the eastern slopes drier.

The big tree, or giant sequoia, has 2" tan, egg-shaped cones and blue-green, scaly leaves with sharp tips.

The Douglas fir has 3–4" egg-shaped cones with bracts that resemble mouse tails. The soft 1" needles have two white stripes on their undersides.

The western red cedar has ¾" leathery scales and flat leaves in fan-like sprays.

The Engelmann spruce has 1–2" cones and 1" sharp, four-sided needles.

The western hemlock has rounded, 1" cones and flat, ½" needles with rounded tips.

The Ponderosa pine has 3–4" cones with prickles on the tips of the scales and 6–8" needles in clusters of three.

● Experience a Rain Forest

On the Olympic Peninsula near the Pacific Ocean, you may find yourself walking in an actual rain forest, often with fog shrouding the treetops overhead. The more common coastal forests include Douglas firs and several kinds of pines, hemlocks, and cedars, or if near water, cottonwoods and willows.

You'll see a lot of green in these woods, in spring and year-round. Most western woods are full of evergreens such as fir, spruce, and pine. These forests are noticeably darker and cooler than eastern forests of deciduous trees.

● Deciduous Forests

Quaking aspen (opposite) is the most common deciduous tree in the western mountains, and the most widely distributed tree in North America, found from coast to coast. Its trunk turns noticeably green in early spring due to the chlorophyll in its bark. Aspen trees are either male or female. The females produce 4-inch-long fruits that look like strings of green beads. The fruits break open in mid-spring, releasing tufted seeds that can travel for miles on the wind. Once established, aspens sprout from roots and can quickly spread to cover large areas.

Bigleaf maple of Pacific Northwest forests, another deciduous tree, is usually found along the coast, near water, and scattered among cottonwoods, alders, and willows. With clusters of sweet-smelling, five-petaled, green-yellow flowers, it is one of the few western trees that are pollinated by bees.

How a Forest Uses Water

Take a walk in the rain to see how a forest makes use of water. First, the rainwater is caught by the leaves of the trees. About 10 percent of that rain evaporates directly off the leaves. Another 10 percent, called *stem flow*, is channeled along the branches, down the trunk, and into the soil, to be taken up by the roots. The rest (called *through fall*) drips off leaves and branches and trickles to the forest floor, carrying nutrients to feed other plants. It flows slowly into the soil and then downhill to join streams and rivers.

Aspen trees appear to quake all over because their unusual flat-stemmed leaves flutter and flap in the gentlest breeze.

New Life on the Forest Floor

You'll see the best show of spring wildflowers and mosses in forest gaps and sunny meadows.

Look on the ground for velvety, lush mosses.

Miner's lettuce has small clusters of flowers held above the leaves. The early settlers gathered it for salads.

The mountain dryas blooms in the Rockies just as the snow is melting. Its white, cuplike flower acts like a solar collector to raise the air temperature. That extra bit of warmth attracts insect pollinators.

Mountain bluebells' delicate flowers start out as pink buds but turn clear blue as they open.

Monarch butterflies leave their winter homes in Mexico and near Pacific Grove, California, and begin flying north to their breeding grounds. Look for them wherever milkweed grows.

● Animals on the Move

As soon as spring comes to western forests, whether coastal or mountain, the animals that live there become more active and begin to move — from south to north and from lower elevations to the heights.

Mule deer and elk now move upslope from their wintering grounds toward high mountain meadows, where they will spend the summer. Brightly hued western tanagers return from Mexico to breed in the coniferous forest. The yellow-bellied marmot emerges from hibernation and roams far from its den to find food.

The golden-mantled ground squirrel awakens from its winter sleep and looks for plants and insects to eat. It resembles a chipmunk without stripes on its reddish head.

mule deer

western tanager

yellow-bellied marmot

golden-mantled
ground squirrel

Frogs a-Courting

Listen for the high-pitched *kreck-ek* call of the tiny **Pacific tree frog**. As soon as the weather warms up, the male starts singing to from low plants growing near water attract a mate. These tiny (less than 2-inch-long) frogs spend most of their lives near the ground, although they do have sticky toe pads that enable them to climb trees if needed.

They are rarely seen because they stop singing when they hear you approaching. They are green to brown (they change color depending on temperature and humidity) with a black stripe through the eye. The egg mass is usually about the size of a golf ball and is laid in temporary pools free of other amphibian eggs. After breeding, the males change their call to a single syllable, *c-r-r-ick*. Near the coast, Pacific tree frogs are active all year round, but at higher elevations they hibernate in the colder months.

The **western toad** does not sing to attract a mate (the call is a chick-like peeping). Instead, the males just hang out near water in the early spring and wait for a female to swim past. Females lay long strings of black eggs that are fertilized by the male. Unlike that of tree frogs, a toad's skin is dry and warty rather than moist and smooth.

Northern alligator lizards, which resemble foot-long, striped alligators, spend their days under rotten logs and rocks.

● Amphibians and Reptiles Are Emerging

During spring, snakes, frogs, salamanders, and lizards awaken from their torpor and come out of their winter hiding places. They bask in warm spots and gradually warm themselves. Until they are warm, they cannot move quickly to escape their predators.

Western fence lizards can be seen defending territories on rocks, logs, and fence posts against other males. The males attract mates by doing "push-ups" to display their bright blue undersides — which females apparently find irresistible.

The foot-long Pacific giant salamander eats creatures like worms that move even more slowly than it does.

western rattlesnake

Western rattlesnakes emerge from their winter dens when the air temperature rises above 50 degrees F. They keep their body temperature between 70 and 100 degrees by either seeking shade or basking in the sun as the air temperature rises and falls, so you may see them in plain view on a flat rock or on the trail in front of you. They often make a rattling sound from the tail when disturbed, and they are poisonous. Keep your eyes and ears open and, of course, do not come any closer than about 15 feet. Here's one creature you really should not touch with a 10-foot pole!

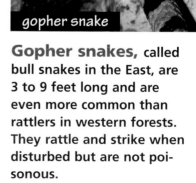
gopher snake

Gopher snakes, called bull snakes in the East, are 3 to 9 feet long and are even more common than rattlers in western forests. They rattle and strike when disturbed but are not poisonous.

garter snake

The common garter snake is usually 1 to 2 feet long with either light stripes or dark spots. It is harmless.

Poisonous or Not?

coral snake

The poisonous coral snake looks a lot like the nonpoisonous California mountain king snake. The difference is in the color bands: red, yellow, black, yellow, red for the coral snake; red, black, white, black, red for the king snake.

To remember which is poisonous, avoid snakes that have red next to yellow, like the color positions in a traffic signal.

King snakes are one of the few predators of rattlesnakes. They also feed on mice.

California mountain king snake

sum

mer

Summer is the best time to explore the woods. The weather is warm or hot, the days are long, and the living is easy for humans and other creatures. There's more to see, hear, and smell than there is in any other season. But don't forget the insect repellent: Summer is bugs' best season, too.

The first day of summer, around the 21st or 22nd of June, marks the time when the sun reaches its maximum height in the sky at noon in the Northern Hemisphere. It also marks the longest day and the shortest night of the entire year.

Now that the trees are in full leaf, the sunlight reaching the forest floor is only 1 percent (or less) of the sunlight in the open, so the forest is far cooler and less windy. But some light does seep in through gaps in the forest canopy. If you're walking on a windy day, watch the moving patterns of sunlight piercing the canopy; the sun's journey across the sky creates moving "sun flecks" across the forest floor.

Summer Weather Report

Local thunderstorms occur throughout the East and in the Rocky Mountains and inland Southwest, but rarely along the Pacific coast.

In the West it's fire season. Low humidity, high winds, and lightning create ideal conditions for a forest fire.

The snowpack is melting in the Rockies and the high Sierra.

The East is often hot, humid, and hazy, thanks to a weather system called the Bermuda High, which brings warm, moist air from the Gulf of Mexico and the Caribbean northward over the eastern states.

What's Up?

Check out what these three creatures are doing in summer.

Black bear mothers roam with their cubs to find food, such as berries.

Cecropia moth caterpillars hatch and *molt* (shed their skin) five times as they grow to between 4 and 5 inches long. They eat constantly all summer long.

Wood frog tadpoles are turning into frogs during summer and can be heard quacking like ducks.

East

Summer thunderstorms are common in the East. Why do they occur more frequently in the afternoon and evening? Thunderclouds build up from warm, wet air rising from the ground. The rising heat and evaporating moisture are most intense during the hottest part of the day, around noon. By late afternoon, everything's ready: The waterlogged air cools rapidly as evening arrives, an electrical charge builds up in the clouds, and . . . kaboom! Lightning. Thunder is the noise caused by the lightning.

● Life on the Wing

Birds wear their brightest colors during the breeding season, so they are easiest to spot in early summer. To see the most birds, time your woodswalk for early morning. Remember? The early birds get the worms.

Watch for a male American redstart, a wood warbler with glossy black head and shoulders and patches of brilliant red and yellow — colors that show up when it fans out its tail as it flits among the low bushes chasing flying insects. Listen for its songs, one a whirring, buzzy sound and the other a high clear squeak.

Many woodland birds stick close to the ground and are camouflaged in browns and grays that make them hard to see. (That's the idea!) The ovenbird, for example, an olive-colored wood warbler, nests and feeds on the ground, where it searches for insects and worms. When singing, it seems to say, "Teacher, teacher."

The veery is a pale thrush, about the size of a robin. Its song sounds like its name. You're more likely to hear one than see one, but when you do, hold still and look for it hopping on the ground, poking among dead leaves for bugs and fallen berries to eat.

The wood thrush is best known for its haunting *ee-o-lay* song, sung by the males in late spring and early summer as they establish territory and advertise for females. Pairs build their nests out of grasses, leaves, pine needles, moss, and mud. Wood thrushes often place something white, such as birch-bark, on the outside rim of the nest.

Nesting Birds

Great blue herons build their nests near water on a platform of sticks, often atop a dead tree.

American redstart females build cuplike nests high above the ground in wooded and swampy areas.

Veeries usually build nests of grass and twigs on the ground near water. A cowbird has deposited its speckled egg here as well.

The ovenbird's unusual nest looks like an old-fashioned bread oven or an upside-down cup, hidden on the ground.

My Bird List

Red Efts

Red efts (the teenage phase of the eastern newt) are easy to see after a rainstorm or early in the morning before the dew has burned off. They begin life as eggs laid in ponds and streams and hatch into *aquatic larvae* — small underwater salamanders with gills. They then turn bright red and crawl out of the water to live on land for several years. Later, as adults, they return to streams and ponds to breed and complete their life cycle.

As water-dwelling larvae and adults their skin is brownish green with red spots. The bright orange-red color of the land phase warns birds that they are poisonous if eaten.

Eastern newts are red only during the land phase of their lives, which may last up to four years. The spots visible on this red eft will remain red and black as it grows into an adult, while the rest of its body turns an olive-brown.

The adult eastern newt returns to the water and lives there for the rest of its life, eating worms, insects, larvae, fairy shrimp, and fish eggs.

You may find red efts among moist plants near the edge of a pond or after a rain along woodland trails. They live throughout the East and Midwest, eating mosquitoes and springtails and spending the winter under leaves and logs.

Life Cycle of the Eastern Newt

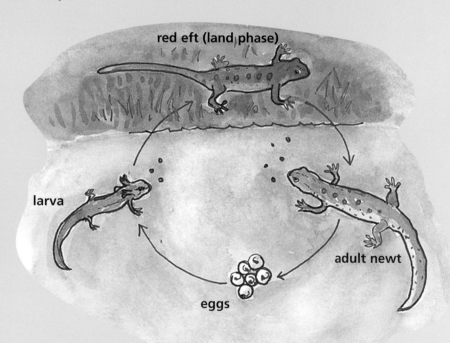

red eft (land phase)

larva

adult newt

eggs

The female newt's 100 or more eggs hatch into aquatic larvae. These crawl onto land as red efts and then return to the pond as adult newts.

Fungi cover this fallen log, feeding off the decaying wood.

● Life in a Fallen Log

Peel away a small piece of bark from a fallen log and you might find the tunnel nests of carpenter ants. These large ants chew at dead wood to build their homes, but they don't actually eat it. This helps decompose the log and turn it into soil.

Summer's warm temperatures and high humidity are perfect conditions for many kinds of fungi to grow. You'll find them on fallen logs, mostly. Look on decaying wood for an oyster mushroom, which is whitish gray and fan-shaped with strongly parallel white gills and a smooth cap.

carpenter ants

oyster mushrooms

The Forest in Bloom

Wild leeks, also called ramps, grow foot-high stalks with clusters of creamy flowers in early summer. Their leaves die back before they flower.

Wood lilies bloom in sunny spots. Their petals point upward but have spaces for rain to drain out.

Harebells, also known as bluebells of Scotland, have small blue, bell-shaped flowers and grow in woodland gaps all across North America.

My Plant List

Wood ferns, like most ferns, have dots on the undersides of their fronds. These release tiny spores, which float away on the wind to make new ferns in moist soil.

● Sounds of a Summer Night

What do you hear in the summer when you stand in the woods and hold very still? Pick out the most noticeable sound at each time of the day. Songbirds are the most likely sound in early morning. In the heat of the afternoon, you'll notice the humming and buzzing of insects, intensifying as afternoon turns into evening.

Mosquitoes are common, but the loudest, raspiest noise will be from the cicada, also called the seventeen-year locust. Toward nightfall, mammals begin to stir, tree frogs sing, and some birds, especially mourning doves and screech owls, may call out.

Cicadas have a loud, sirenlike song, rising and falling in pitch, at dusk and during the day.

Crickets chirp in a steady pulse, faster on warm nights and slower on cool nights.

Katydids are named for their night song, a shrill "katy-DID." Some also say "katy-DIDN'T."

Bug Box

Dig around in the soil and look for millipedes, which are *detritivores*, meaning they eat dead organic matter such as fallen leaves. Good thing, because otherwise the woods would fill up with old dead stuff. Also watch for centipedes, which are larger, with fewer legs. Don't pick them up: they are carnivores, and they can bite.

Grasshoppers rub their hind legs along their wings to make a low, rasping sound. They sing during the day.

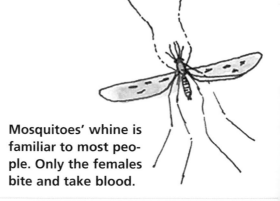

Mosquitoes' whine is familiar to most people. Only the females bite and take blood.

Fawns start following their mothers when they're five weeks old. They lose their spots at four months old.

● Mammals in Action

Many different kinds of mammals are busy during the summer, raising their young and eating as much as they can to store up fat for the fall and winter, when food will not be so plentiful. The best times to watch for mammals are very early in the morning and late in the evening, during the first and last hours of daylight. The less noise you make (and that includes talking!) and the less you move around, the better your chances of seeing some animals in action.

This is the time when fawns — the gangly baby deer with the distinctive white spots — will be following their mothers around. They are curious and may not yet have learned that one of their best defenses is to stand completely still. If you spot a fawn walking around, browsing, don't go near it. Its mother is sure to be nearby.

Family Time

During the summer, animals teach their babies how to find food, whether by hunting, fishing, grazing, or browsing. Foxes, for example, whether red or gray, teach their pups to hunt small animals like rabbits and mice, so that when they go off on their own in the fall, they will be able to feed themselves. The striped skunk is a nighttime hunter in handsome black and white stripes. You may smell one before seeing it. Do not approach or disturb it.

If you're near a large pond, be alert for beavers. Summer is when they build dams and their domed lodges. Look for gnawed stumps of small trees — a sign of busy beavers. Watch also for weasels and mink. Both animals are long and thin (weasels are brown in summer, mink are very dark brown with fine coats) and den up near water. Both hunt at night for small animals, birds, eggs, mice, and frogs.

Mother skunks stroll with their babies to teach them how to catch prey.

Weasel families hunt together during the babies' first summer.

Mink parents catch fish for their young.

Gray fox pups become self-sufficient by summer's end.

● A Seldom Seen Cat

There's one forest resident that lives all over North America, in probably every wild place you may visit. Read about it here, because you'll probably never set eyes on . . . a bobcat.

Large wild cats — not only the bobcat, but also the cougar or mountain lion and the lynx of northern forests — are very rarely seen in the wild, even by experts. That's because these animals hunt stealthily at night and are seldom active during daylight hours when hikers are in the woods. Bobcats wait quietly for small animals, like mice and rabbits, to pass by, and then they pounce.

Bobcats are loners. They live in a group only when the mother is still caring for her two or three cubs in a den under a rock ledge or a fallen log.

All you may see of a bobcat in the woods is its tracks, especially in winter snow or spring mud. They look a lot like house cat tracks, only larger, with four toes and a "heel" showing, but no claw marks visible. Each print is 1 to 2 inches across and will appear generally in a straight line, though each is set a little bit to the left or right.

Bobcats belong to the same family as house cats, but are larger and heavier than even the biggest pet. Their black-tipped tails are short —bobbed — and their ears are more pointed than those of a domestic cat, with small tufts of fur at the tips. Their colors and markings are excellent camouflage and make the cat almost invisible.

West

In the higher mountains of the West — the Sierra Nevada, the Cascades, and the Rockies — the winter's deep snowpack is finally melting. The snow at the highest levels may not vanish completely, and in places above the tree line, you may even find small glaciers. The melting snow pack is an important source of water for all forms of life downstream.

Along the Pacific coast and in the mountains inland, summer is a dry season, with less rainfall than in winter and spring. The dry, rising air can create "heat lightning" — that is, thunder and lightning without any rain. Heat lightning often starts forest fires.

Fire is not just destructive. It is also important to the life of the western forests. The cones of giant sequoias and lodgepole pines, for example, are glued shut with pitch until they are opened by the heat of a fire. Only then can their seeds sprout. Quaking aspen and fireweed return rapidly to the burned area as they thrive on the nutrients in the ash. That burned area will later become a forest with nearly all the trees the same size and age.

Fireweed is one of the first plants to reappear after fire, volcanic eruption, logging, or any other disturbance. Its magenta flowers produce lots of downy seeds that can travel hundreds of miles on the wind.

● Forest Superlatives

A walk in the western woods can place you in the shade of the largest, tallest, or oldest trees on the North American continent. The big tree (sometimes called the giant sequoia) grows to enormous size and age in fewer than 100 groves along the Pacific slope of the Sierra Nevada. The trunks of the big trees can be 10 to 12 feet in diameter.

GENERAL SHERMAN

Senior Citizens

The "General Sherman" big tree in Sequoia National Park (left) is called the largest tree in the world. It's as tall as a 27-story building and its base is as wide as a three-lane highway. The oldest tree in the world is a bristlecone pine in the White Mountains of eastern California, the so-called Methuselah tree (below), at about 4,760 years old.

Coastal redwoods grow in a 30-mile-wide strip along the Pacific coast.

Along the central California coast, you can walk in a grove of old-growth coastal redwoods, and there is no mistaking this forest for any other. These trees live long and grow tall — up to 300 feet and higher. The world's tallest tree is a coastal redwood in California that reaches above 360 feet. With massive straight trunks and a vaulting structure of branches far overhead, a redwood grove may remind people of a great cathedral.

How Water Travels through Trees

Water enters the tree from the soil and moves up the trunk through the branches to the leaves. (In coastal redwoods this may be a climb of more than 300 feet!) It evaporates from tiny pores on the undersides of leaves, which pulls up more water from the soil in a process called *transpiration*. In deciduous forests, transpiration stops in autumn when leaves fall. This means woodland streams often have more water after leaves have fallen.

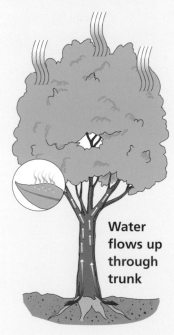

Water flows up through trunk

Tree Nursery

When walking in the forests of the Pacific Northwest, look for what are called "nurse" logs — large logs fallen over and covered with mosses and lichens. The mosses and lichens can provide an ideal seedbed for tree saplings, not too dry and not too wet. You may see a row of tall trees growing right out of a huge, horizontal nurse log.

● Mountain Fragrances

Wildflowers go on a blooming binge in the higher mountain meadows during the summer. The fragrant bright yellow or whitish flowers of glacier lilies appear as snow recedes up the mountain. Colorado columbine's large blue and white flowers bloom in aspen groves and woodland openings in the Rockies. The pollinators of summer wildflowers — whether bees, flies, ants, hummingbirds, or moths — must work long days visiting the abundant blooms.

Wildflowers such as elephant heads (whose flowers resemble tiny pink elephants) grow in wet mountain meadows. They flower just as worker bumblebees emerge from their winter nests. The bees nestle against the pink "trunks" and at the same time beat the air violently with their wings, dusting themselves with a cloud of pollen. They then repeat this process on other flowers to cross-pollinate them. Without bumblebees, we would see no pink elephants.

When the air is damp after a rain, it's easier for the human nose to smell what's in it. The air can be a bouquet of several aromas. Sharp odors may be ozone from lightning or acid from the rain. Sweet, earthy scents are a mixture of rock and soil compounds called *petrichor,* along with bacteria spores in the soil. Chemicals in leaves are washed off by rain showers and may add subtle odors to the air.

Bursting into Bloom

| Colorado columbine | glacier lilies | elephant heads |

The wildflowers found in high meadows look fragile but are sturdy enough to withstand mountain winds and freezes.

Banana Slugs

Summer is the easiest time to see banana slugs, as they are most "active" during warm-weather nights in the Pacific coast forests. They come in a wide range of colors — gray-brown, pink, and, of course, banana yellow. They are related to snails but without shells, and they grow much larger, up to 10 inches long. In the redwood forests they favor, they eat living or recently-dead plant material (or even animal dung). To get around, slugs glide along on a trail of their own slime. They are protected by their slime, which allows them to glide unhurt over sharp edges like broken glass.

Slug slime also plays a part in the mating ritual. They sense the presence of another slug by chemical signals in the mucus trail and will often eat their partner's slime. Then they mate, engulfed in their mutual slime.

Rather than having eyes, slugs have light detectors on the tentacles atop their heads (they can't really see). A mantle covers the head end of their bodies, and on the right side of this mantle is the slug's breathing hole.

Slug slime is one of the world's best glues, and with its help slugs can stick to tree trunks, fingers, twigs, and each other.

● An Underwater Bird

Water ouzels, or American dippers, are very active songbirds of the Pacific states. Their loud metallic warble continues from winter to early summer, when the streams they live near dry up. Dippers are unusual birds because they forage beneath the water of fast-flowing (even whitewater) streams to eat insect larvae. They don't have webbed feet but instead use their wings to "fly" underwater. Their heavy coat of feathers insulates them so they can feed in very cold water, remaining submerged for up to a half-minute.

An ouzel nest is unusual too: a rounded affair made largely of moss and located on rocks at streamside.

The water ouzel can dive, swim, and walk along the bottom of swift streams.

● Look and Listen

You might see elks, moose, mule deer, beavers, porcupines, bighorn sheep, and mountain goats in the summer woods. Other animals, such as cougar, wolverine, lynx, and marten, are active but so elusive that you would be very lucky to spot one. This is the time when you are most likely to catch a glimpse of a bear. It will most likely be a black bear. Grizzly bears are found in or near Yellowstone and Glacier National Parks and northwest from Alberta to Alaska.

Moose will be enjoying their favorite foods, the succulent plants that grow on the bottom of ponds. They wade out, duck their heads under the water, bite off these "pond weeds," and raise their heads to chew and swallow. You may encounter a moose with growing antlers covered in a downy velvet. The ones with antlers are bulls (males). The females, as well as the young calves that often accompany them, have no antlers. Keep your distance. These are large, heavy, surprisingly fast animals that do not like being approached by people.

Bears have a keen sense of smell, so keep any food you're carrying tightly sealed, and if you're camping, keep food well away from your tent site. If you know there are bears nearby — if you've seen fresh tracks or *scat* (poop) — sing loudly or whistle or rattle your gear so the bears, who don't see well, won't be startled by your approach. Be sure to travel in a group in bear country.

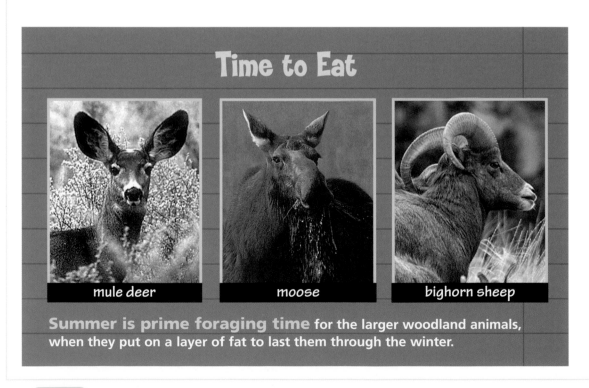

Time to Eat

mule deer

moose

bighorn sheep

Summer is prime foraging time for the larger woodland animals, when they put on a layer of fat to last them through the winter.

black bear cubs

If you do meet a bear, especially a mother with cubs, back away slowly, and don't make any sudden moves. Talk softly and soothingly to the bear. If it's a grizzly bear, look for a nearby tree to climb. Black bears are good climbers, but grizzlies are not.

Don't approach a bear, especially a mother with cubs. If she thinks you are a threat, she will attack you.

• What Not to Do When You See a Bear

Do not run. Despite their fat, shambling appearance, bears move faster than you can run, and they are like dogs; if you run, they will chase you.

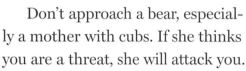

grizzly bear

pika

The pika, a small, frisky mammal of the high mountains, spends a busy summer in clearings, harvesting goodies for winter. Pikas gather wildflowers, grasses, and seeds, roll them into tiny piles, and pull them down into their dens for use in the winter. They make a bleating sound but look like small-eared, miniature rabbits. Pikas often have a second litter of "pups" during the middle of the summer. If you don't hear them, you can locate them by looking for the white stains of their dried-out urine on their rocky homes.

● A Hammer for a Beak

During the summer, many forest-dwelling birds are active and noisy. The Clark's nutcracker, a relative of the crow, harvests unripe seeds from closed pine and fir cones by jabbing its bill between the cone scales or by removing the entire cone and taking it to an "anvil" station where it hammers away to release the seeds. Then it places the seeds in a pouch under its tongue and flies off to store them in "caches" of as many as 15 seeds, which may be several miles away. By fall a single bird may store thousands of seeds.

Clark's nutcracker

● Taste Summer Berries

Serviceberries, or Saskatoon berries, are tasty and may have received their common name from the U.S. cavalrymen eating them in the late 19th century. Chokecherries are quite sour but can be used to make jam. Black raspberries, red raspberries, and blackberries ripen in that order. The red-orange salmonberry grows only in Pacific coast forests and is really yummy. All are delicious. Thimbleberry, with white flowers in the West, has large, flattened, beautiful fruit but it's not as juicy as other berries.

Steer clear of baneberries, both red and white. They grow in clusters on plants about 1 to 2 feet tall, but are bitter-tasting and poisonous.

WARNING: All parts of the red baneberry are poisonous to humans, although not to birds and small mammals. Its close relative, doll's-eyes, has white berries with a single black dot on them and may be growing close by. It is also poisonous.

Hank Says

Berry Confusing

Is it a black raspberry or a blackberry? As you pull the fruit from the stem, look inside the berry where the stem was attached. If you see an empty hole, it's a black raspberry; if the hole is filled with a white plug, it's a blackberry. Both are delicious.

Berries Galore

chokecherries

raspberries

blackberries

thimbleberry

autu

mn

Autumn is the most colorful season of the year for a walk in the woods. Summer greens change to brighter reds, browns, yellows, and golds. After the leaves turn colors, they "fall" from the trees. Of course, that's the other name for this season — fall.

Two important activities go on in the animal world in autumn: migrating and mating. Birds, some bats, and monarch butterflies fly south in the autumn to avoid the coldest weather. Deer, elks, and moose all mate in this season, and that calls for caution. The males are now aggressive and just plain ornery as they compete — even battle — for the females. So when you see any of these big animals, keep your distance.

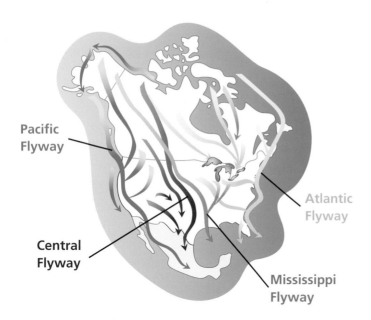

Pacific
Flyway

Atlantic
Flyway

Central
Flyway

Mississippi
Flyway

Not all birds migrate, but about 150 different species do. They tend to follow the four major north–south routes known as *flyways*.

Autumn Weather Report

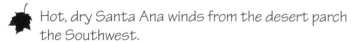 If you walk early in the morning in late fall, you may see a white coating on leaves, grasses, tree trunks, rocks — almost any surface close to the ground. That's frost, sometimes called "hoarfrost," and it forms when the surface temperatures drop below 32 degrees. Frost is just condensed, frozen fog. In summer, it would be dew.

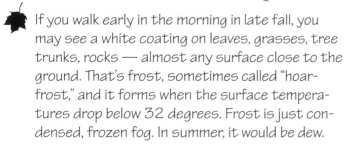 In fall the Aleutian Low weather system brings rainstorms to the Pacific Northwest from the Gulf of Alaska.

 Hot, dry Santa Ana winds from the desert parch the Southwest.

 In the Southeast, hurricane season reaches its peak in October.

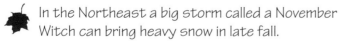 In the Northeast a big storm called a November Witch can bring heavy snow in late fall.

East

Leaf colors vary from year to year, depending on the weather. When nights are clear and cold and days are bright and sunny, the colors will be brilliant. When nights are generally warm and days are dull and rainy, however, the fall colors will be duller than usual. In most parts of the East there may be more rain in the fall, so be prepared for a wet woodswalk. The leaves underfoot may be slippery, so wear boots that grip, especially on a rocky trail. When the woods are wet, you can smell more of the forest scents.

In the Southeast near the coast, this is hurricane season, the time when powerful storms form over the tropical waters of the Atlantic Ocean, the Caribbean Sea, or the Gulf of Mexico. And several times a season, these storms can come blasting onto the mainland.

● Look for Signs of Fall

Not all trees change color at once: It's an uneven process, and in the early fall you can see that each leaf changes gradually. Some leaves will be part green, part yellow, part red, and part brown. Return to the same spot a week or two later and look again at the color changes. Collect some fallen leaves and try to figure out which trees change color first.

woolly bear

Woolly bears, the hairy, black-and-brown-striped caterpillars, are the larvae of the yellow-brown Isabella tiger moth. Unlike most butterflies and moths, woolly bears overwinter in the caterpillar stage of their life cycle. Legend has it that the length of their colored bands in the fall predicts the severity of the upcoming winter. In reality, the bands tell us about their previous growing conditions — more brown and less black just means it was a good summer.

Leaf List

Leaves turn colors when they stop producing green chlorophyll at the end of the growing season, revealing the yellow pigments that have been there all along. Red, orange, and purple pigments are produced in the fall, especially when nights are cool and days are sunny.

COLOR	TREE TYPE
Yellow	aspen, birch, box elder, cottonwood, hickory, silver maple, tulip tree, witch hazel
Red	black gum, hornbeam, red maple, scarlet oak, sumac
Orange	sassafras, sugar maple, sweet gum
Brown	beech, chestnut, sycamore, some oaks
Purple	dogwood, maple-leaved viburnum, white ash

Amazing Fliers

Birds are capable of traveling incredible distances in their yearly migrations. Many of the smallest songbirds, like the gray-and-white-striped blackpoll warblers of northern forests, migrate the farthest. They are known to fly hundreds of miles over the open ocean, flying day and night for 72 hours at a stretch, all the way to Brazil.

Flocks Are Gathering

Watch for large mixed flocks of birds that settle suddenly in the trees. During migration and winter feeding, different species of birds travel and feed together. Insect-eating birds may pass quickly through a wooded area in pursuit of flying insects, but seed eaters may stay longer, feeding on tree trunks and digging into bark. Some birds that stick around all winter begin to flock together in the fall, probably for group protection.

Red-winged blackbirds often travel with starlings and grackles in large, noisy groups.

● Look Down at Decomposers

In autumn, as many as 10 million leaves per acre will fall and pile up in a thick layer on the floor of a deciduous forest. They are not only beautiful, but they are also essential food. They become food through decomposition: that is, the process of breaking the leaves down into the chemicals that compose them, and thus providing nutrition to other kinds of plant and animal life. It is one of nature's biggest recycling projects.

The invisible creatures that do most of the work of turning autumn leaves into rich soil are bacteria, protozoans, and fungi. They are helped by larger creatures that live in the "litter layer" of the forest — insects, mites, millipedes, isopods (those familiar pillbugs), earthworms, various beetles, and even moles — all of them feeding on and breaking down those leaves.

Return to the same area next spring and you'll see how the thick layer of leaves has been matted down by rain and snow. Visit again in late summer to see how much decomposition has occurred. Notice that some leaves, like oak, decompose more slowly than others, such as maple.

Mistletoe

When leaves have fallen, mistletoe, with its leathery, wedge-shaped, evergreen leaves, is more visible in the treetops, most commonly in southern forests. It is a *parasitic* plant — its roots tap into the host tree for water and food. Mistletoe's sticky seeds are transported from tree to tree attached to the feet of birds.

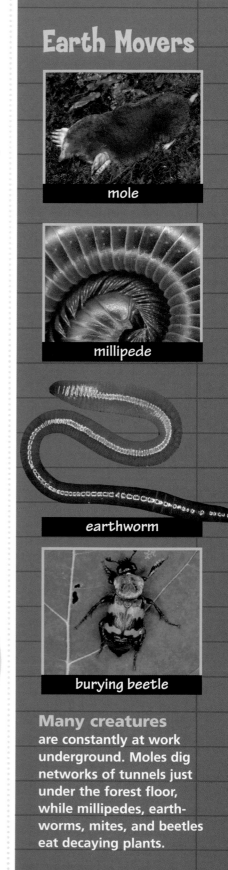

Earth Movers

mole

millipede

earthworm

burying beetle

Many creatures are constantly at work underground. Moles dig networks of tunnels just under the forest floor, while millipedes, earthworms, mites, and beetles eat decaying plants.

Fungi Up Close

Autumn is the peak season for all kinds of mushrooms, and if you walk after a rainfall, you'll see them everywhere. Many types of fungi — life-forms that feed on rich soil and fallen logs — spring into view in the autumn. What we see on the forest floor are their "fruiting bodies" rising from underground. Instead of seeds, fungi produce *spores* for reproduction, which are spread by the wind. When the forest is bare of leaves, the spores spread more easily.

scarlet cup

chanterelles

coral fungus

rainbow bracket fungi

Look on dead wood for scarlet cup fungi and the colorful bracket fungi that grow like shelves on trees and logs. Chanterelles are vase-shaped and often come in bright colors. Coral fungi look like ocean coral growing on the forest floor.

stomping a giant puffball

giant puffball

Giant puffballs first appear firm and white in summer and turn brown in autumn. They can be as small as a baseball or as big as a basketball. If you tap the top of a dry brown puffball, you'll see a smokelike wisp of spores puff out. Stomp on one to release an explosive cloud of several trillion spores. But do not taste or eat mature puffballs — they contain poisons.

Please Don't Eat the Mushrooms

Many types of mushrooms make great eating, but many others are highly poisonous. What's more, the good ones and the bad ones often look alike. Even if you're sure you can tell the difference, play it safe — don't eat any mushrooms you find in the woods.

Amanita muscaria (poisonous)

● Quiet Sounds of Fall

A few frosty nights will have stilled most of the insects and amphibians of summer, so an autumn twilight in the forest will be quieter. Once leaves are on the ground, stand very still, especially near a pond or animal trails, and listen carefully. The rustling dry leaves make it possible to hear animals and birds moving around. Even a chipmunk now makes quite a racket when dashing over and among the leaves. Listen for larger animals as well as they prepare for winter.

Nose for Nuts

Listen for the popping of witch hazel fruits. **This plant blooms in the fall, with yellow, stringy flowers that take a full year to produce their woody capsules. The capsules snap open when ripe, making a clicking sound. When they pop open, they can shoot the seeds up to several yards.**

If a squirrel can't remember where it buried nuts in the fall, it can often find buried food by smelling it. Squirrels are known to smell acorns under as much as a foot of snow!

witch hazel

hickory nuts

In fall, male white-tail and mule deer polish their antlers against trees to remove the flaky velvet. Look for saplings with the bark freshly scraped away. At the end of the breeding season the males shed their antlers. In winter and spring, small mammals gnaw on the cast-off antlers for nutrition.

Chipmunks stuff seeds and nuts in their cheek pouches before stashing them.

Small mammals in the Northeast hide hickory nuts and acorns among the stones in old stone walls and along fence lines, which often gives rise to a new row of hickory and oak trees. Here is a cache in a rotted log.

Collecting Fall Leaves

Most of us collect leaves by colors and put together a bouquet of reds, oranges, yellows, and browns. But instead, try collecting leaves by the different shapes. Walk from one type of tree to another and pick up the best examples you can find. Then compare them to the pictures on these pages to find out what kind of leaves they are.

Beech leaves, like oak leaves, linger on the trees well into the winter.

Gray birch leaves are more tapered and pointed than beech leaves are.

Oak leaves are large and leathery with many lobes and a single main vein. After turning brown, many will stay on the tree till spring.

The main veins of maple leaves are arranged like the fingers on your hand. Red maple leaves (left) have V-shaped indentations and jagged outside edges.

Sugar maple leaves have U-shaped indentations and smooth outside edges.

Ash leaves are *compound*, meaning that seven or more leaflets share a single stem.

Sumac leaves have toothed edges and more leaflets per stem than ash leaves do.

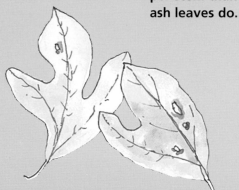

Sassafras leaves are shaped like mittens, with smooth outside edges.

Hank's Hints

Telling Conifers Apart

How can you tell a fir from a spruce from a pine? Here are some tips.

FIR needles are flat and soft, so if you touch them, they won't prick you. Remember: "friendly fir." Their cones fall apart during the winter. Their buds are globe-shaped and often sticky.

fir

SPRUCE needles are stiff and sharp. Their cones have scales that stay attached after the seeds are gone. Their buds are cone-shaped, too, and scaly.

spruce

PINE needles are mostly longer and grow in bundles of two to five needles along each twig.

pine

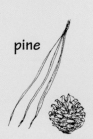

My Favorite Leaves

West

Western forests are made up mostly of evergreen trees, especially in the mountains, so you won't see the brilliant fall colors of eastern forests. Evergreen trees and shrubs do drop their slender needles. Except for pines, though, most drop them a few at a time all year round and not all at once in the fall, the way deciduous trees do. That's why there is almost always a carpet of brown needles, slowly decomposing, on the floor of a conifer forest.

● Leaves of Gold

The big splash of color in the West comes from quaking aspen. A deciduous tree that grows throughout the northern forests and all over the mountain West, aspen is a medium-sized, fast-growing poplar with creamy white bark. Growing in groves in the Rockies, aspen can color entire mountainsides a bright golden yellow. The sunlight on a large grove of yellow-leafed aspens, quaking and shimmering in an autumn breeze, is a not-to-be-missed sight.

If you're in an aspen grove that's near a pond or a stream backwater, look for gnawed aspen trunks. Beavers like aspen both for food and for dam-building materials.

Why Do Leaves Fall?

Days are shorter and nights are cooler than in summer. That's the cue for deciduous trees and shrubs to produce a chemical that forms a brittle, corky layer between each leaf and its twig. Once the leaves are no longer firmly attached to the tree or shrub, a hard frost, a rainstorm, or a high wind will bring them down.

Liquid water is scarce during the winter, so trees and other plants respond by withdrawing their nutrients into their stems (their trunks) and roots, shedding their leaves, and closing down for the winter.

Preparing for Winter

The blue grouse moves upward toward higher elevations, seeking dense conifer thickets for its winter home.

The pine siskin migrates south in large flocks.

Long-Distance Royalty

Every autumn, the familiar orange-and-black monarch butterflies, flitting and fluttering around the edge of a forest or around your backyard, migrate surprising distances. In the West, they flock together and spend the winter on California's Monterey peninsula.

Even the youngest monarchs, several generations removed from the ones that flew north last spring, still find their way instinctively to the same few winter spots.

The golden-mantled ground squirrel tirelessly collects seeds and insects until the first snows fall, and then goes underground into its burrow.

Signs of Winter

● Mating and Migrating

In fall, elks migrate down from the high mountain meadows where they have spent the warm weather grazing and bulking up for the fall mating season and the rigors of winter. Traveling in herds of about 25 animals, they are most active in the dim light of dawn and dusk. Now they are eager to find partners and mate, or *rut*. The females will give birth to one or two spotted calves in spring.

Like deer, the bulls scrape their antlers against the woody branches of small trees to rub off the velvet; look for freshly scraped bark to see evidence of elks passing through. By now their antlers have reached full width. The largest elk antlers on record are more than 6 feet from tip to tip.

Bull elks often bugle as summer turns to fall. Their calls start low, build to a high-pitched warble, and end with low grunts.

Clashing Antlers

During mating season male elks fight with each other, "jousting" with their antlers to win a harem of females.

coho salmon swimming upstream

grizzly bear fishing

Like elks and birds, some fish migrate, too. Along many coastal streams and rivers in the Northwest from September through November, chinook and coho salmon migrate from the ocean up the same stream where they were born years before. Upstream they *spawn* — that is, they deposit their eggs — and then die. Salmon is a favorite catch, not only for humans but also for bears preparing for their winter snooze: They need to build a layer of fat to get through the cold season.

On your autumn walk, look for fruit on all the plants, from the tiniest herbs to the biggest trees. When we think of fruit in the fall, mostly we think of apples on trees and pumpkins on vines. But many plants produce fruit in this season. From the plants' point of view, the fruit is a protective package for their seeds. Examine plants of every size and see if you can find the fruit. Look for wild grapes on vines, and for the berries on such shrubs as red elderberry, holly, and sumac (holly and sumac are red and easy to spot). A good way to find fruit on trees or shrubs is to watch the migrating birds. They know where the berries are. So do bears, which fill their bellies before winter sets in.

Flash Power in a Plant

Club mosses, small creeping plants that are more closely related to ferns than to true mosses, release their clouds of yellow, powdery spores in autumn after the leaves have fallen. Touch some of them along the trailside to see plumes of spores floating off on the breeze. The fine, powdery spores have been used in cosmetics and once were used as flash powder prior to the invention of flashbulbs and electronic photo flashes.

club moss

wild grapes

red elderberries

holly berries

sumac

ter

Winter is a great time to walk in the woods, even if the ground is covered with snow. With the trees and shrubs bare, you can see farther into the woods and notice the land and its shapes.

Better make it a short walk, though. There's not as much daylight in winter, and the shortest day of the year occurs around the 21st of December. The cooling and the heating of the land, air, and water always lag behind the sun's movements by about a month, so the coldest days of the year happen in late January to early February.

• Winter Weather Report

❄ In the East, cold air is surging southward from northern Canada, while ocean-born storms called Northeasters often bring heavy rain, heavy snow, and severe coastal flooding.

❄ Dry, frigid air from the Canadian Rockies flows southeast across the Great Lakes in a weather system called an Alberta clipper.

❄ A northeastern winter has high winds and snow; rain is more likely in the Southeast.

❄ Ice storms can occur throughout the East, even in Florida.

❄ Western storms arise in the Pacific Ocean. Every few years there is an El Niño cycle, when warmer than usual ocean waters cause record rainfall along the Pacific coast and in the South.

❄ Winter means rain on the Pacific coast, while there is snow in the mountains and in the interior.

What's Up?

Check out what these three creatures are doing in winter.

Black bears snooze in a warm den. Cubs are born while the mother sleeps.

The cecropia moth pupa is resting for the winter, enclosed in a large, papery, 4-inch cocoon.

Wood frogs are in hibernation, burrowed under leaves on the forest floor.

East

The eastern forests present shapes and contrasts in winter: small creeks and outlines of ponds; boulders and other rock formations; and the terrain, more visible now through a screen of bare branches. It's a good time to observe the shades and patterns of tree bark, as well as the colors of twigs and buds on trees and shrubs. The pines, firs, and spruces up top, plus the rhododendrons, holly, and wintergreens closer to the ground, are most noticeable.

● Look into the Past

In the bare woods it's easy to see where earlier uses of the land left their marks. You can spot trails made by animals or by people, or the twin tracks of old logging or farm roads. Look for the remnants of stone walls or old fence lines and even old plow lines, all left over from times when most of the woods had been cut down by settlers and what is now forest was crop fields and pasture.

plow lines

Old-Growth Forests

There are still some old-growth forests remaining, even in the East, and usually in state parks or state forests (they are far more common in the West). Sometimes called "virgin forests," these are stands of trees that have never been cut down, so the trees are very old and often very large. In Pennsylvania, for instance, there are 19 stands of old-growth forest. Others are in Maine, New Hampshire, Vermont, Massachusetts, Virginia, North Carolina, Georgia, and Florida.

Some beech trees hold on to their dead leaves for almost the entire winter.

● Winter Branches

In winter you can see the overall shapes of the trees. Irregular shapes and broken-off branches may record a past ice storm that bent or even broke the branches. Birch trees — especially paper birch and gray birch — in young forests often show signs of bending by heavy snow.

Many deciduous trees look dead at this time of year, but of course they're not. Most are in a state of *dormancy* — that is, water and sap are not moving from the roots to the leaves as they do at other times of the year. Many trees require a dormant period in winter in order for their buds to burst the following spring.

A Guide to Tree Buds

TREE	BUD DESCRIPTION
Red maple	small, globe-shaped, red scales
White oak	gray twigs; small, globe-shaped, yellow-tan scales
White ash	look like milk-chocolate chips
Tulip tree	look like brown mittens without thumbs

red maple

white ash

white oak

tulip tree

Winter Nest Spotting

A bluejay nest is of ragged construction, usually found in an evergreen. Diameter: 7–8 inches.

A gray squirrel's summer home is a leafy mass. Its winter home is a hole in a tree. Diameter: about 2 feet.

A red-winged blackbird's nest is low and found near water. Diameter: 3 inches.

A robin's cup-shaped nest is made of twigs, mud, and, sometimes, animal fur. Diameter: 6½ inches.

A crow's nest, found high in the fork of a tree, is made of sticks, unlike a leafy squirrel nest. Large and bulky, it may include cornstalks, string, and cloth as well as bark, roots, grasses, and moss. Diameter: about 2 feet.

A red-eyed vireo's nest is tiny, made of bark, grasses, and spider egg cases, and lined with plant down. Diameter: 3 inches.

My Nest List

A song sparrow's nest is made of grasses, bark, and leaves and found on the ground or in a shrub. Diameter: 5–9 inches.

When trees warm up in the sun, they melt the snow immediately around them. Bowl-shaped depressions then form around the bases of the trunks.

● The Quiet Sounds of Winter

At this time of year in the woods, you may wonder where everybody went. You won't hear the buzzing of insects or the peeping of amphibians, or nearly as many bird calls and songs. Some animals that were busily collecting food are now hibernating; others are finished with noisy mating battles. All is quiet.

On a windy day, you may hear the squeaking of tree trunks and branches rubbing together. Although trees don't usually freeze in winter, with a sudden drop in temperature ice crystals may form in the cells within a tree trunk or branch. On a very cold evening, you may hear cracking sounds from nearby trees, as those ice crystals explode and the outer bark shrinks rapidly.

Listen for the tapping and knocking of wood-peckers searching trees for insects. On still winter nights, sounds carry long distances through the woods. You may catch the shriek of a bobcat or the soft call of an owl.

Listen for flocks of birds. In winter, several of the smaller species like chickadees, creepers, titmice, and sparrows gather together and stay in one territory to search for food. Pine siskins and goldfinches (now dull olive-green) often flock together, and they're pretty noisy about it. They call to communicate and stake out a feeding territory in the woods.

The great horned owl is a superb night-time predator, thanks to its excellent hearing, night vision, and silent flight. The best time to see or hear an owl is on a calm moonlit night. An owl pellet (below) consists of the undigested bones and fur of its prey. If you find one on the snow, look up: The owl's roost may be in the tree above.

owl pellet

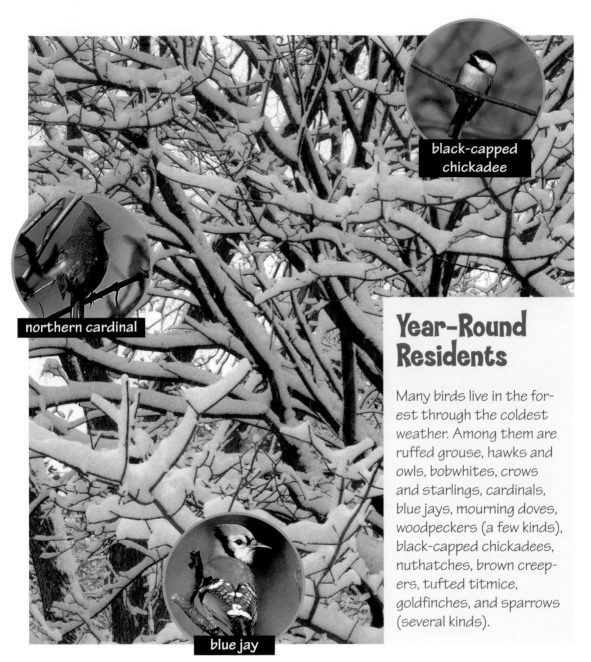

black-capped chickadee

northern cardinal

blue jay

Year-Round Residents

Many birds live in the forest through the coldest weather. Among them are ruffed grouse, hawks and owls, bobwhites, crows and starlings, cardinals, blue jays, mourning doves, woodpeckers (a few kinds), black-capped chickadees, nuthatches, brown creepers, tufted titmice, goldfinches, and sparrows (several kinds).

Because food is less plentiful — especially when snow is blanketing everything — winter birds are very active during the day, searching hard for food, mostly for insects and seeds. They shiver a lot as a way of keeping warm. You may notice them fluffing up their feathers: That's how they increase the thickness of their insulation to save body heat and keep warm. At night, some of the small birds, like black-capped chickadees, enter what's called a *state of torpor*, when their body temperature can drop nearly to the freezing point of water. In the morning, they warm up again.

Winter Fungi

Hard brown bracket or shelf fungi are easy to spot in winter.

Conch fungus grows on trunks and stumps.

Artist conch, which grow to several feet wide, have soft undersides to their caps, which turn brown when scratched.

Black knot fungus often grows on cherry twigs and looks just like hardened dog poop.

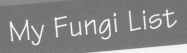

My Fungi List

Animal Tracks

The best thing about snow in the woods is . . . tracks. The ideal time to read these tracks is in the morning after a light overnight snowfall. Then you can see what animals were moving around at night, where they went, and perhaps where they live.

If you have the boots, the time, and the patience, follow one set of tracks. They may lead to food, water, or shelter, or to the end of the story, where blood, feathers, or fur in an area of kicked-up snow tell you that predator met prey.

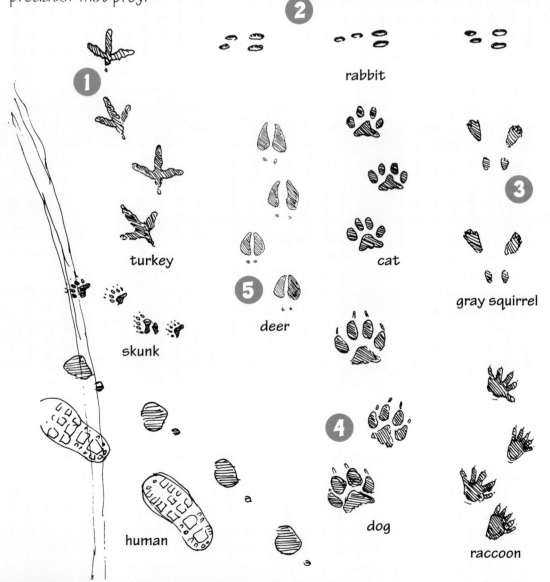

turkey

rabbit

cat

gray squirrel

skunk

deer

dog

raccoon

human

1 **Most of the larger birds** walk, while smaller ones tend to hop, leaving different pairs of tracks. Sometimes the tracks suddenly begin or end — that's where a bird landed or took flight.

2 **When rabbits are moving** quickly, their tracks are farther apart. They spring forward and land on their front feet, then plant their longer hind feet in front and leap again. It's an easy pattern to see. Is the rabbit being chased? Look for other animal tracks following the rabbit's.

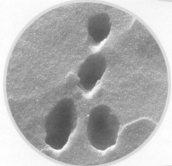

3 **Squirrels and mice** often move from tree to tree. Their tracks may include the line of a dragging tail. See if any of the tracks lead to a hole, which could be a burrow.

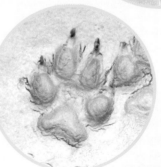

4 **Nearly all canine,** or dog-family, tracks look alike. The tracks of a fox are smaller than those of most dogs, however, and almost always very straight; dogs wander and sniff and play, while foxes appear to stick to their business. You can often see the marks of toenails in canine tracks, unlike tracks of the cat family.

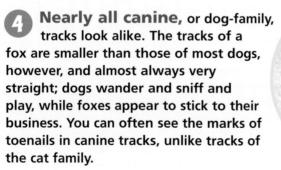

5 **Deer wander through the woods** in a winding path as they browse among shrubs and saplings. You may see marks on tree trunks where they have nibbled at bark.

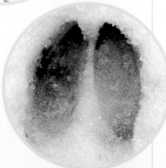

ermine

vole

snowshoe hare

Some animals, like snowshoe hares and weasels (their winter name is ermine), change color, turning white and becoming harder to see in snow.

● Life in the Snow

Animals that live in snow country adapt to their surroundings. The ruffed grouse grows "combs" on its feet that work like snowshoes and let it run without sinking into the snow. Deer can't run well in snow, so they stay in deer "parks" or "yards," grouping together in the shelter of thick stands of conifers, especially spruce trees, where the overhead branches keep the snow from the ground.

When the snow gets deep enough, some animals use it in other ways. Mice, shrews, and voles tunnel under the snow at ground level, so they can move about and feed without being spotted by predators like owls and keep warm under the layers of snow. In late winter or early spring, when the snow melts, you may find the clear paths of a large network of mouse-size tunnels laid bare.

● Look Closely at Winter Insects

winter moth

The woods are quieter in winter than in other seasons, but that does not mean that all insects are dead and gone. Winter moths are active, especially on a warm day. These tan moths mate during the winter. You may see honeybees on the surface of the snow in early winter. These are dying drones, pushed out of a hive by the more essential worker bees.

Few insects are active in winter. Most either lay eggs and then die, overwinter as cocoons, or burrow into the ground. All insects are cold-blooded, and most survive winter's cold by coming to a complete halt, a state called *diapause*. During a warming trend, they will become active. Look for signs of insects' homes: galleries carved by bark beetles, nests of wasps, galls on the stems of goldenrod and willows.

When the air temperature falls below freezing, the water in the soil also begins to freeze. You may see, along the edges of a trail, ice prisms or even little ice columns that push up through the bare soil. These prisms, caused by soil moisture freezing and expanding upward, even lift up small pebbles, which look like caps on top of the ice columns.

Snow Fleas

Sharp-eyed woodswalkers may spot snow fleas, tiny wingless insects, on the snow. They show up most clearly on the snow, even though they live in the woods all year. Snow fleas, a kind of springtail, feed on algae, fungi, and bacteria on the snow. They gather in large numbers, and sometimes on a warm day fresh tracks and footprints can be filled with them, drinking the melted water and eating their micro-scopic food.

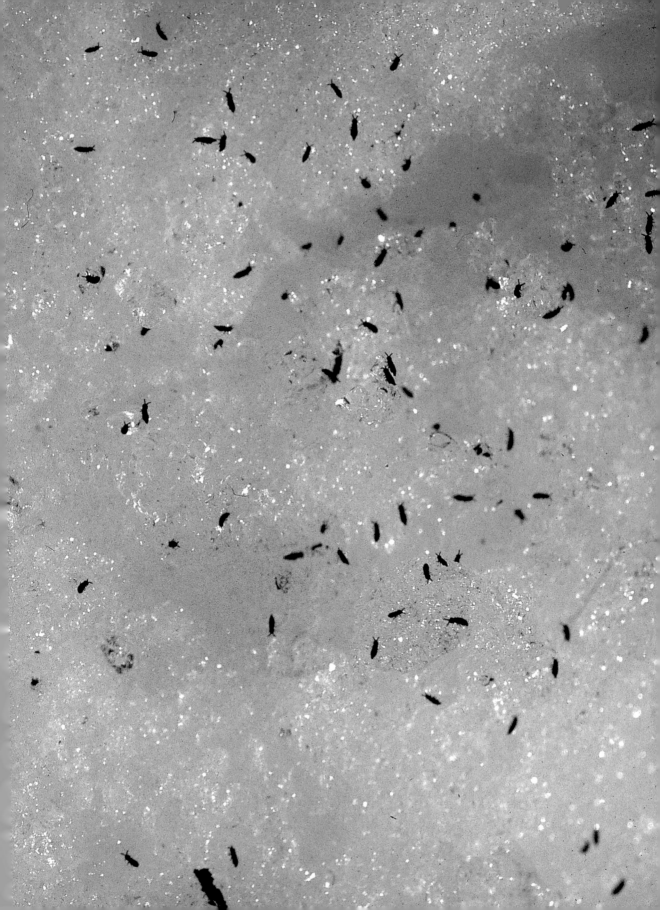

West

In a western forest, a winter walk could be a mild-weather stroll, a slog through the rain, or a snowshoes-only romp in some very deep snow, depending on where you are. Along the central California coast and in the coastal rain forest of the Pacific Northwest, a winter walk will be a lot like a spring or fall walk. The temperatures will be mild and the forest doesn't look very different from season to season.

If you're walking in the Cascade Range or the Sierra Nevada, however, you'll encounter snowfalls as early as October. There's usually about 10 feet of snow on the ground on any winter day.

● Look Up into the Treetops

Away from the coasts and higher in the Sierra Nevada and Rocky Mountains, conifers are the most common type of tree. Even though they stay green through the harshest winters, the spruces, pines, firs, and cedars stay dormant until spring.

After a heavy snowfall, look at how the snow collects on tree branches. Conifers such as spruces and firs have cone-shaped crowns that shed snow like a peaked roof. Pines are not so cone-shaped, but have bendable branches that flop down to shed the snow and then spring back up. That way, the heavy snow does not break down the trees.

Avalanche!

In the mountains an avalanche (a collapse of the snowpack) may occur when deep fresh snow covers slippery, icy layers. It roars down mountainsides at more than 200 miles per hour. As an avalanche grows it can sweep away trees, cabins, and every other object (including you) in its path. When it finally stops at the bottom of a slope, the avalanche may be 40 to 100 feet thick.

avalanche in Denali National Park

Moose don't hibernate, but stay in conifer thickets where the browsing is good.

● Coping with the Cold

Snow is important for plants and animals because it makes great insulation. The temperature on the ground under a snowdrift could be as much as 25 degrees higher than the outside air temperature. If the snow has come early and stayed all winter long, the soil beneath it may stay unfrozen. Some plants and many small animals are protected from damage by this layer of snow.

In very deep snow, you could dig a snow cave with a shelf to sit on and the temperature inside the cave would remain about 38 degrees — slightly above freezing — no matter how cold it got outside. That's how people can live in igloos without freezing.

Listen to Winter Tunes

Mountain chickadees often forage in conifer forests for winter insects.

Dark-eyed juncos have a twittering, ticking call. When they start to migrate, they sing a long, trilling song.

White-crowned sparrows have a high, thin, almost whispering whistle.

Golden-crowned kinglets are small and elusive but deliver a surprisingly loud, reedy *eee-eee* call.

Birdsongs

The water ouzel or American dipper sings its loud, metallic warble from winter until early summer.

gray wolf paws

● Staying Warm

Did you ever wonder why the feet of warm-blooded animals don't seem to freeze to the snow? Birds' and mammals' feet do get cold on the outside, often falling below freezing temperature, but apparently the animals don't mind. The blood flowing toward the feet is cooled by the blood flowing away from the feet. Their foot pads are insulated by thickened skin, fur, fat, and a kind of "antifreeze" compound to keep their feet from freezing.

The gray wolf, now limited to the far north country, stays warm thanks to its dense underfur.

Go on a Woodland Treasure Hunt!

Every season there are different things to look for in the woods.
How many of these can you find?

What to look for in spring:

- baby animals (don't touch!)
- frogs or peepers calling
- vernal pool
- flowers on a tree
- butterfly, moth, or caterpillar
- bird singing
- woodpecker tapping
- beaver lodge
- woodland wildflower
- fiddlehead

What to look for in summer:

- tadpoles
- bird's nest
- red eft
- fungus-covered log
- fern
- cricket chirping
- baby animal with its mother
- woodland wildflower
- slug
- edible berries

What to look for in autumn:

- flock of birds
- woolly bear caterpillar
- a two-colored leaf
- millipede or earthworm
- colorful mushroom
- butterfly, moth, or caterpillar
- puffball
- acorns or other fallen nuts
- wild grapes
- small mammal gathering nuts

What to look for in winter:

- old stone wall in the woods
- tree buds
- bird's nest
- trees creaking and cracking
- a woodpecker tapping
- mushrooms
- animal tracks
- signs of insects
- pine, spruce, or fir cone
- flock of birds looking for food

Glossary

boreal forest. A type of forest containing mostly coniferous trees that stretches across northern North America and in mountainous terrain farther south. Also called *the Northern forest.*

camouflage. Protective coloring of animals that allows them to blend in with their surroundings and avoid being spotted by predators.

canopy. The top layer of a forest, created by the overlapping leaves and branches of the tallest trees. Full sunlight strikes the tops of canopy trees.

carnivore. An animal that eats other animals for its food. Wolves, bears, and mountain lions are carnivores.

chlorophyll. The green coloring found in leaves and other green parts of most plants. Chlorophyll absorbs sunlight, which is used in photosynthesis, the way plants make food for themselves. (For more details, see *photosynthesis.*)

cold-blooded. Describes animals whose body temperatures are similar to the temperature of their environments, so animals in a hot climate grow warm and animals in a cold climate grow cool. Most insects, reptiles, and amphibians are cold-blooded, also called ectotherms.

community. A group of organisms of different species living together in the same area.

cone. The woody seed holders produced by trees like pine, spruce, and fir.

coniferous. Describes trees that produce woody cones. They are usually evergreen and have needle-shaped leaves.

cross-pollinate. To transfer pollen from a flower on one plant to a flower on a different plant of the same species. This is the important job bees perform by flying from one flower to another.

deciduous. Describes plants that drop their leaves at the end of each growing season. (Evergreen trees drop some needles, or leaves, all year long, but never drop them all at one time.)

decompose. To break down, rot, and decay, usually through the action of bacteria and fungi.

detritivore. An animal that eats dead organic matter (anything that was once alive, whether animal or plant) as its source of food.

diapause. A period of dormancy that some insects enter to escape extreme environmental conditions.

dormancy. A condition of suspended activity, especially during winter. Both plants and animals can be dormant.

evaporation. The action of changing from a liquid to a gas without boiling. If you leave a small cup of water out in the summer sun for a day, the cup will be empty when you check on it later. The water in the cup has evaporated into a gas and mixed with the air.

evergreen. Describes trees and plants that keep their green leaves or needles throughout the year.

fiddlehead. A fern frond that uncurls as the leaf is emerging from the ground in the spring. Many different species of ferns have fiddleheads.

foliage. All the leaves on one plant or in a group of plants (window box, backyard, or forest).

forage. To look for plants and parts of plants to be used as food. We usually describe animals as foraging, but if you go looking for blackberries or dandelion greens, you're foraging, too.

frond. The leaf of a fern or palm.

fungus. An organism that obtains its nourishment by absorbing food and reproduces by producing spores. Mushrooms and yeasts are fungi (pronounced *fun-guy*).

gall. A growth or swelling on a plant caused by insects, parasitic bacteria, or fungi.

gill (mushroom). The thin, radiating structure that bears spores under the cap of a mushroom.

glacier. Sheet of ice that forms when the snow accumulating over winter is greater than can be melted during the rest of the year.

herbivore. A plant-eating animal. Deer and moose are herbivores.

hermaphrodite. An organism that is both male and female. Many species of plants have flowers with both male and female sex organs. Earthworms are animals that are hermaphrodites.

hibernation. A sleeplike condition during winter in which activity is reduced, metabolism is reduced, and body temperature can fall to near that of the air (down to a degree or so above freezing).

humidity. The amount of moisture (water vapor) held in the atmosphere (air).

hyphae. Long threadlike parts that form the underground bodies of fungi, especially mushrooms. One would be called a *hypha*.

insulation. A layer of material that slows down the escape of heat from an organism or the ground.

larva. Immature stage of many organisms, such as tadpoles, grubs, and caterpillars, which will grow up into frogs or toads, beetles, and butterflies or moths.

lichen. An "organism" that consists of two other kinds of organisms — algae and fungi — living together.

life cycle. The complete series of changes that an organism undergoes during its lifetime. Many insects — butterflies, for example — completely change their appearance during their life cycles.

migration. The seasonal movement of groups of animals from one region to another and back again.

old-growth. A mature forest that has had little or no logging or grazing.

omnivore. An animal that eats both plants and other animals for its food.

Bears and raccoons are omnivores. Many if not most humans are omnivores.

organism. A living being, whether plant or animal.

overwinter. To survive from autumn to spring. Some plants overwinter, but others die and are replaced by all-new plants in the spring.

parasite. An organism that gets its food from another living organism but without killing it. The food-providing organism is called a host.

photosynthesis. The way in which plants change light, water, and carbon dioxide into sugars and oxygen. The sugars are food for the plant. The oxygen is released for the air-breathing animals on the planet.

pigment. Coloring substance in an organism. The colors of animal fur and plant leaves are produced by pigments.

predator. An animal that hunts down or traps live animals (prey) for its food. Wolves and coyotes are predators.

prey. An animal that is eaten for food by a predator. Prey are usually herbivores. Rabbits and mice are prey.

raptor. A predator bird that obtains its food by killing live animals (prey). Hawks and owls are raptors.

scat, a.k.a. poop. The unused food waste excreted by animals.

spawn. To lay eggs directly into water, as fish and frogs do.

spores. Reproductive cells produced without the joining of sex cells and capable of developing into new organisms.

terrestrial. Describes organisms living on the land (rather than in a watery environment).

torpor. A state of reduced activity for a short period of time, such as overnight. Hibernation and dormancy last much longer, usually for months.

transpiration. How water evaporates from the surface of plants (leaves and stems) into the air.

tree line. An invisible boundary line near the tops of very high mountains. Below the line, the conditions allow trees to grow. Above the line, conditions are too harsh for trees, although other lower vegetation may still grow.

warm-blooded. Describes animals that regulate their body temperatures by producing heat through metabolism. Birds and mammals can keep their body temperatures constant even when the temperature of the environment changes dramatically. Also called endotherms.

Other Books to Read

Golden Guides

Zim, Herbert Spencer, and others. *Trees: A Guide to Familiar American Trees.* The Golden Guide Series. St. Martin's Press, 2001. Other highly recommended Golden Guides include *Insects, Birds, Mammals, Wildflowers,* and *Reptiles & Amphibians.*

National Audubon Society Field Guides

Little, Elbert L., Jr. *The National Audubon Society Field Guide to North American Trees.* Knopf,

1980. Other guides in this series focus on birds, mammals, insects and spiders, butterflies and moths, and reptiles and amphibians.

Peterson Field Guides

Kricher, John C., and Gordon Morrison. *Peterson First Guide to Forests.* Houghton Mifflin, 1999.

Wehr, Janet (illustrator). *Peterson First Guide to Trees.* Houghton Mifflin, 1998.

Wehr, Janet (illustrator), and George A. Petrides (author). *A Field Guide to Eastern Trees.* Peterson Field Guides. Houghton Mifflin, 1998.

Interior Photo Credits

Illustration Credits

Index

An *italicized* page number indicates a photograph or illustration; **boldface** means the information appears in a chart.